Learning to Sing

A Transformative Approach and Instr...

by Jennifer F

Chapter One

Introduction

For over fifteen years, I have had the privilege and pleasure of performing and teaching in the field of music at the professional level. During that time, I published my first book, *The Art of Singing: Discovering and Developing Your True Voice,* which not only discusses my experiences as a singer and a vocal coach, but also shares my thoughts on the proper approach to training vocalists and their voices.

The desire to capture my ideas about vocal instruction and execution stemmed from years of noting a vast chasm in many singers between intellectual understanding of vocal technique and performance outcome. This gap between 'knowing' and 'doing' seemed further expanded by emotional issues directly and peripherally related to voice production and performance. In fact, an inverse relationship often existed between the intensity of conscious intellectual and emotional investment in singing well and the ability to do so.

These areas of inquiry– intellectual, emotional, and somatic– have traditionally been perceived and treated as distinct concepts. Voice teachers and instructors of pedagogy focus on the comprehension of vocal technique. Psychologists and therapists deal with the myriad emotional issues that arise in the study and practice of the performing arts. Vocal coaches and directors concern themselves with performance outcome.

On the surface, this segregated treatment makes sense. Given the mastery of their specializations, it seems logical that these professionals would focus largely, if not entirely, on their specific areas of expertise, leaving others to deal with what appear to be associated or even unrelated matters.

Unfortunately, this compartmentalized approach rarely leads to a collective resolution. Vocal technique that is theoretically comprehended but not consistently manifested is just as ineffective– and common– as a highly skilled singer who crumbles in the face of performance anxiety. Both are akin, as a non-musical reference, to emotional and psychological issues that are understood, but unable to be shifted or resolved.

By addressing intellectual, emotional, and somatic concerns in specific and simultaneous ways, however, significant change in vocal ability is not only possible, but predictable. What's more, the cognitive and emotional strongholds that once prevented progress– both related to music and not– unravel as well.

In these chapters, I'll distinguish this integrated approach that I have developed in my practice, beginning by addressing the three areas of inquiry– the mind, emotions, and the body– and their common, individual roles in the vocal learning and performing contexts. I'll then explore how to access the powerful and transformative interplay between them, followed by discussing the applicability of this approach for achieving optimal outcomes in other areas of learning and life.

Chapter Two

Intellect

The Unqualified Advocate

The first issue in the disparity between vocal knowing and vocal doing relates to the intellect's trouble translating information in a way that can be wholly integrated into somatic expression. Indeed, the best explanations of technique by teachers– and conscious understanding of them by students– often do little to help singers incorporate these facts into predictable and effortless physical action.

It's not that the efforts of the teachers or students are lacking. It is that the intellect and its messenger– language– are simply not designed to understand and command, respectively, what is first and foremost a reflexive physical engagement.

As a non-musical point of reference, consider the processes of walking, talking, and standing up. While the conscious mind knows that these actions are possible and predictable, and has an awareness that they are occurring, it makes no attempts to actively engage, manage, or technically understand the intricacies of their functioning. In these instances, the physical-first processes are allowed to occur unbothered and unchecked.

For an experience of what would be an intellect-led course of action in these areas, try instructing someone precisely how to walk, talk, stand up, or to sit down. What you will find is that the conscious mind has tremendous difficulty pinpointing, in both directing and describing, the myriad muscular movements and engagements required to achieve these physical outcomes. If we want to stand, we simply stand; attempts at explanations generally prove to be exercises in frustration and futility.

So it is with singing. Just as we are able to speak without a conscious thought every day, so too do our singing voices function automatically. Certainly the mind is able to initiate, observe, and make modifications to the process as it does with speech; just as we can choose to begin a sentence, to speak more loudly, to imitate someone, or to put on an accent, so too may we choose to utilize more resonance, to increase our volume, to straighten a tone, or to shift into a different vocal register. Yet, in speaking and singing alike, these choices– when effective– manifest to a large extent on their own; we do not consciously implement them muscle by muscle.

The automatic design and nature of the voice, both in singing and speaking, may be better understood by considering the mechanism of breath support. The muscles responsible for inhalation and voiced, supported exhalation are too numerous, varied in placement, and intricate in functioning to consciously command in their entirety. What's more, much of the system is also reflexive in its engagement, meaning that we are unable to directly activate aspects of it.

The diaphragm is an excellent case in point. Enabling inhalation, this dome-shaped muscle below the lungs engages automatically (thus, our ability to breathe while sleeping). During our waking hours we can certainly observe that the diaphragm is engaging, optimize the conditions for its functioning through mental and physical relaxation, and even assist the respiration process by actively taking in air. Still, we remain unable to deliberately cause it to independently engage.

To make matters more complicated, we are also unable to actually feel the diaphragm, along with other aspects of the vocal mechanism. This is thanks to proprioception– a form of internal physical perception related not to the 'feeling' and nerve-based orientation with which we're familiar on the outside of our bodies, but rather, to a spatial sense of orientation based upon stimuli within the neuromuscular apparatus and body itself.

Learning

In spite of these and other factors that prevent us from consciously engaging, holistically controlling, and even feeling aspects of the vocal mechanism, many still approach singing in precisely this intellectual manner. The discussion of 'actively engaging the diaphragm', for example, is common in current training programs, academic methodologies, and voice publications around the globe.

There are a number of reasons why the intellect has been elevated to a role of such supreme power in the current voice training paradigm, including the introduction of music to high school and university curricula. Yet the folding of the vocal arts into the academic model did more than provide new opportunities for students. It necessarily, if not unintentionally, required the teaching methodology to conform to the current education and instruction standards as well.

Unfortunately, realizing the physical engagement of singing is distinct from the study of music's academic aspects (for which the intellect is a good fit). The latter model traditionally involves, as it does in non-music classrooms, a primarily unidirectional transfer of cognitive, fact-based information from teacher to student. Given that it is the mind that is first and foremost being addressed, this transfer also implies a passive physicality on the part of the learner, rather than the participatory action so necessary to both comprehend and integrate certain– and certainly physical– types of knowledge.

Setting aside what they physically know, vocal students are then made to wait for instruction to engage specific musculature that is often unable to be consciously engaged, felt, or initiated independently. As you might imagine, these efforts tend to result not only in improper engagement, but in frustration, confusion, and other emotional responses to the failure of correct action.

Language

Before speaking to these responses, as well as to a number of common emotional issues in singing and voice training, a closer look at the role of language in the vocal learning process is required.

As a request for (or a reflection of) physically autonomous action, language is in its proper and helpful role. Just as we automatically respond when asked to stand or sit, so too can language evoke in us the engagement of, modifications to, and development of our singing voices.

However, in the mind's effort to actively control the vocal mechanism, language serves as more hindrance than help. Disconnected by the intellect from the inherent and wordless physical knowing, the body has no choice but to rely on a bridge of linguistic cues and clues for how to engage. As such, language becomes a tool of direct command, in spite of the fact that many such requests are unable to be actively or accurately manifested in the body.

To illustrate this point, consider a recent conversation (or read this paragraph aloud). Recall the laughter, the way you emphasized points at certain moments, or may have questioned your speaking partner's words at others.

Looking back, we recognize the presence of vocal modulations. We observe and can describe that our voices moved 'higher' at certain points and 'lower' at others, that we 'breathed' at the start of certain phrases, and utilized a variety of 'tones' during the course of the conversation. This linguistic commentary is a reflection of the obvious, of what has already occurred– of what was accomplished largely unconsciously and automatically.

Yet when we attempt to speak or sing through a line with the intention of actively commanding these modulations in tone, breath, pitch, and the like, the process ceases to be effortless; subtle and not-so-subtle tensions begin to emerge. We notice that it now seems an awkward challenge to make certain sounds and to move our voices 'up' and 'down', where before we were vaguely, if at all, aware of these modulations or our thoughts about them.

Part of this comes from the previously discussed inability of the intellect and language to deliberately cause what are, for the most part, reflexive engagements. Yet an equally important issue is that the linguistic cues we are using are largely or entirely unrelated to physical reality.

For example, our entire conceptual notion of pitch is based on a related scale of up and down. Yet while the words 'high' and 'low' describe the directionality of notes as they appear on a musical staff, they are not correlated to our biology. The vocal folds, resting in the larynx, vibrate faster and slower for 'high' and 'low' notes, respectively. They move neither up nor down in accordance with our linguistic or graphical representation.

Were we to simply use the words 'high' and 'low' as reflections of an acknowledged and trusted physical reality, this wouldn't be a problem. But again, when somatic knowing has been intentionally or unintentionally set aside, the body responds to language by attempting to literally create its requests. This results in singers reaching 'up' for 'high' notes with their efforts and energy– as well as with their throats, their eyes, their chins, their necks, and their eyebrows– in spite of the fact that these actions do nothing to help and much to hinder the desired intent of achieving 'high' notes.

This misleading notion of up and down is not an anomaly in the musical language. The entire spectrum of vocal engagements, modulations, and modifications– high, low, bright, dark, support, placement, head and chest tones, and even the demarcating and naming of notes– are linguistically either inaccurate or semi-accurate when considered from the physiological vantage point. When taken as literal commands, rather than cues to trigger instinctive or reflexive physical processes, these words cause an active narrowing and focusing of energy, as well as the participation of unnecessary musculature, which then limit the vocal mechanism from its proper engagement, producing the opposite or certainly different results from those desired.

Belief and Judgment

Rather than propel vocalists to consider an alternative approach to voice production, these intellectual, learning-related, and linguistic difficulties paradoxically confirm and reinforce the struggle. Just as inaccuracies in and reliance upon language hinder the achievement of optimal vocal engagements, so too do incorrect ideas about singing spring to life, become culturally empowered, and then limit what is actually possible. These ideas include that singing is difficult, that only a few people have the talent required to sing well, and that it takes a tremendous and even strenuous amount of effort to do so.

No matter how true these ideas might appear, a look at other cultures– as well as certain members of our Western society– reveals that this isn't the case. It is the beliefs about singing and the specialness of one's voice, rather than the inherent quality of the voice itself, that largely determines both who sings and how well they do so. Indeed, members of various traditional, agrarian-based, and spiritual cultures– as well as children from around the world– sing with an effortlessness, beauty, and joy that seem downright impossible given our own societal agreements and beliefs.

Impossible as it may appear, this type of relationship with singing is a birthright we all share. It only seems otherwise because of the cultural education we begin receiving as children; education that hinders natural physical development. It is this education– rather than the accuracy of its message– which causes us to unlearn the ease of singing we all once knew and to surrender the voice that belongs to each of us.

To compound the issue, we in the West not only assign a high qualitative value to musical expression, but to the individuals creating that expression. We deem as worthy and special those few who are perceived to have talent, adding additional pressure to those desiring to express themselves.

This pressure further engages and empowers not only the intellect, but also the mind's judgmental and ego-related aspects. Thus empowered, these facets of the mind then inhibit the ability to optimally engage in the processes of singing and learning to sing, regardless of what is physically possible. In a vicious cycle, frustration mounts as attempts to intellectualize, control, and over-personalize physical engagement result in diminished vocal returns.

Chapter Three

Emotion

In addition to the challenges presented by the intellect, language, and beliefs, singers and teachers of singing must also contend with issues relating to emotions and emotional health. While the theoretical understanding and physical production of the voice may seem largely unrelated to these concerns– save perhaps for those associated with confidence and performance anxiety– they are entirely relevant and indeed, interrelated.

Our bodies are road maps of our emotional and psychological wellness or lack thereof. In the voice as in the body, somatic expressions of these issues– while not necessarily comfortable or effective– are present according to the conscious and unconscious beliefs and perceptions relating to our current, past, and anticipated experiences.

The slight bowing of the head or puffing of the chest that might speak to sadness and false pride, respectively, are non-musical equivalents to what singers present in vocal quality, production, regulation, tone, breath, posture, and overall functioning of the voice in response to a variety of emotional and psychological factors. These 'markers' are present in virtually every singer to some extent; the voice is therefore as much a demonstration of prior vocal training and inherent understanding as it is a survey of issues relating to the self, including self-in-world, self-in-system, and self-as-singer.

While vocalists are generally very in touch with how they feel about their voices, they are often surprised by the connection between their emotions and their physical experiences of singing. Even greater is their surprise at the ability of emotions– particularly those not seemingly related to singing– to so powerfully affect, manifest in, and even control voice production and learning.

Given this powerful correlation, emotions and the beliefs they inform must be addressed if healthy self-expression is to be achieved. Voice teachers are therefore put in a position to necessarily deal with the emotional issues and stressors of their clients, both related and unrelated to singing, whether in active discussion or in the management of the unspoken effects.

Common Issues

To illustrate how emotionality frequently plays out in the voice– both in performance and instruction– it is helpful to consider a few common issues.

Perfection, Adequacy, Confidence

Many singers experience a struggle with perfectionism, concerns regarding adequacy– vocal and otherwise– and the 'right' to self-express. As is often the case of many limiting perceptions of self, these issues inadvertently become the focus of expression in spite of conscious efforts to the contrary. Longing to achieve far more in their singing than a high-quality physical engagement– including, but not limited to, validation and self-protection– singers wrestling with these matters generally stifle their voice production in one of two ways.

The first is through a presentation of an overabundance of energy and effort in singing, a vocal proving of sorts. Pushing and straining in an endeavor to enlarge or perfect voice size and quality is common, as is the 'pushing' of mental and vocal energy toward the intention of pitch and tonal perfection. Both are tools that singers use in their often unconscious attempts to hide perceived artistic and personal failings, as well as in an effort to control both voice production and others' reactions to it.

Conversely, fears of inadequacy often present through constriction– the holding of the breath and the tightening around higher and louder notes, as well as in more emotionally charged musical pieces, are two such common engagements. Areas of the voice or songs that a singer imagines to be difficult or vulnerable become off-limits, in actuality or commitment, due to the perception of their challenging or revealing nature.

Certain physical manifestations– the pushing of the voice in self-proving, the holding of the breath in self-protection– appear to be logical somatic extensions and expressions of emotional concerns. Physiologically, however, even these seemingly opposite vocal aims produce startlingly similar results. Tension, ineffective use of breath, lifting of the larynx, and other improper engagements are present in each of the aforementioned cases, in spite of the differences in both the vocal and emotional intentions.

What's more, these psychologically associated voice issues often aurally present quite similarly to problems stemming from vocal fatigue, injury, illness, and allergy– presentations that themselves evoke emotional responses. As such, it is imperative to be able to tease apart the somatic and emotional roots of causation, lest a teacher incorrectly address a physical issue that exists because of an emotional one, or vice versa.

Shame, Guilt, Anger

Matters become increasingly complicated when longstanding psychological issues not directly related to singing and performance begin to manifest in the voice. Shame, guilt, anger, and other emotions make themselves firmly at home in a singer's vocal production in frequently unexpected and unpredictable ways. Anger, for example, may masquerade as a tentative or quiet voice– perhaps for the imagined consequences of expressing it or for fear of losing control– often causing a secondary emotional reaction to an undesired or even loathed vocal timidity.

A singer on the brink of emotional overwhelm, on the other hand, might manage a consistently beautiful and powerful performance through dissociation. While the helpful and even enviable constancy often provides for the avoidance of performance anxiety and a reprieve from the emotional unrest it often inflicts, this 'skill' puts the singer at risk for a performative or emotional break that could render her vocally and personally devastated both in the moment and beyond.

Failure and Success

Finally, fears of failure and success are two common issues, both of which can arise in fascinating ways at any stage of a vocalist's journey. Highly intriguing are those who have performed effortlessly and consistently throughout their careers, only to encounter vocal troubles at the most professionally inconvenient of times.

In these cases, it is not only vocal and emotional tension, but also structural vocal issues that are common. Skeletal asymmetries and muscular strains, acid reflux, and vocal nodules, hemorrhages, and polyps are typical physical presentations that bring these singers to a halt. With such tangible evidence, it seems– and often is– impossible to embark on a scheduled tour or to begin the recording of an anticipated album.

(Of course, it is imperative to note that these same tension and structural issues can and do often occur as independent physical matters, with no causal emotional component. Incorrect and over usage of the vocal instrument, as well as diet, fatigue, and illness lead to these presentations frequently. Here, we are specifically discussing the role emotion can play with respect to certain vocal issues.)

While their physical issues are clear to doctors and voice teachers alike, there is very often a longstanding psychological component lurking beneath the surface, exacerbating or even causing the physical one. Singers arrive to medical and vocal appointments desperate to resolve the barriers that stand between them and the continuation of their careers, entirely unaware that they themselves have perhaps had a hand in the creation of the issues for which they are seeking help. The last thing on their minds is that they could be unwittingly sabotaging themselves, their performances, and even their voices in order to avoid the risk of failure or success.

Yet this is precisely what so often happens. The question is why, and more, how can these singers be unaware of what is going on?

Commitment to Stasis

To answer these questions, we must consider the relationship of human beings to the notion of change, as well as what it is that fundamentally guides us in our decision-making.

While talent and passion are certainly factors, there are many issues– both conscious and unconscious– that propel us into careers, relationships, and other life circumstances. And despite what we might think, our fears, limiting beliefs, and unhealthy patterns are often just as powerful and motivating as our aptitudes and interests.

When decisions are made with both in play, as they so often are– talent and a concern about worth, passion and fear– the chosen field or relationship is not only a source of pleasure. It is also responsible for fulfilling the greater aim of our personal validation.

In the vocal realm, these singers therefore find themselves serving two masters: passion for music and performance, as well as the simultaneous proving and protection of the self.

Because of these dual, generally conflicting and– regarding self-proving and self-protection– often unconscious aims, motivation and intention are never clear. Intense as a singer's desire may be for a quality and successful performance outcome, it rivals the equally powerful commitment to the perception of safety, leaving her in a vocal and personal standstill.

This dilemma not only results in frustration and fear. By fascinating and ironic extension, it leads to and often creates the very vocal, technical, and performance challenges that singers desire to avoid. Physical issues and injuries arise on cue as manifestations of fears of failure and success, insecurities, and the like. The higher the stakes– as in the example of the aforementioned touring and recording artists– the more willing a singer is, albeit unconsciously, to compromise vocal integrity in the face of both challenges and opportunities.

Instead of prompting an objective consideration of the roots of causation, these physical issues in fact encourage singers to cling more strongly to their emotions. The feelings and fears that *preceded* the vocal issues are now perceived by the panicked singer as a *reaction* to the compromised vocal experience. Given this perception, frustration seems like an entirely appropriate (and emotionally safe) reaction; working hard to uncover a solution to a physical problem feels like a more empowering place to stand than looking into and acknowledging any anxieties about personal worth, failure, or success.

Thus a relationship with compounded layers of emotionality is formed and forged against what appears to the singer to be technical or structural vocal issues rather than what they are in reality: physical manifestations created and held in place by the singer's own initial fears.

This helps to explain the very personal relationship singers and performers often have with their emotional experiences, regardless of whether or not these experiences help them in the pursuit of their conscious aims. Many singers come to voice coaching with these relationships firmly intact in both mind and body, hoping to gain information so that they *together* might move forward. Implied in this way of thinking is that their emotional commitments are not going anywhere. The notion that they must– or even can– be left behind is often incredibly confusing and even disconcerting.

The Rewards of Non-Change

This ineffective, yet common dynamic can best be understood through the lens of reward theory, which supposes that our actions are given less by our objective desires and intentions and more by the benefits– conscious or otherwise– that we are receiving for either pursuing or resisting them.

While familiar to many in the psychological field, this is generally a foreign concept to those in the performance realm, who imagine that the only desired 'rewards' are those of vocal and performance success. After all, when the entirety of one's conscious effort is spent improving technique and furthering a career, the notion that a benefit from *not* achieving the purported aims seems inaccurate and even offensive.

Regardless of their perceptions, singers have attachments to the majority of outcomes they are achieving, in spite of how undesirable those outcomes might appear to them. This is true for everyone and in every area; whether we're aware of it or not, our current circumstances are largely the result of decisions we've made and continue to make for the resultant rewards we receive.

There is no question that life can be unpredictable and with its challenges. Yet a critical look reveals that while our goals and intentions may be certain and sincere, they are– when they remain unachieved– generally less powerful than our desire to sustain certain practical or emotional elements of our current situations. In this way, the woman who tries but fails to return to school and the man who longs for but is unable to secure a meaningful relationship have a tremendous amount in common with the singer who wants to perform, but does not manage to book any engagements. All three may long to achieve their goals. Yet if their fears and concerns remain greater than their desires, so too will success remain elusive.

The Perils of Emotion Management

Because of the intense relationships many singers have with their emotions and the stasis-related rewards surrounding personal and performance outcomes, even the most adept and capable vocal teachers struggle with their resolution. Common approaches, while logical and sensible in theory, frequently fail to move emotionality to the periphery in order to secure the ultimate goals of voice production: clarity, creativity, comfort– both physical and emotional– and consistency.

Comprehension

The first strategy many teachers employ is to engage singers in a conversation about their presenting emotional issues. Unfortunately, in addition to taking time away from vocal work, attending to the emotions often serves to empower them.

Understanding might be achieved on an intellectual level, but does little to alleviate the cause and dominance of emotion in vocal production and performance.

Negotiation

Similarly, teachers and coaches will often use comprehension in an effort to facilitate a negotiation between emotional experience and desired physical outcome. This creates a conversation that leverages an understanding of what the emotions mean and why they are there against the importance of moving them to the periphery in order to achieve performance and career goals.

Unfortunately, while a greater amount of causal detail may be available in this scenario, voice production will not shift so long as the established reward structures remain in place. Rewards are visceral and emotional rather than logical in nature; a conversation about the greater aim of success or joy in performance will not supplant the current goal. Therefore, the emotionality of the singer remains, possibly now further empowered for the amount of discussion about and number of failed attempts at altering the dynamic.

Avoidance

Finally, teachers will often avoid the issue of emotion entirely, whether for a lack of interest, knowledge, or belief in its ability to affect instruction. While this approach ensures that attention is focused on the voice, it doesn't necessarily lead to greater vocal progress. Training can only be somewhat effective without an acknowledgment– at least on the part of the teacher– of any related reward structures; technical work alone will not overcome what is indeed a commitment to tension.

In addition to stagnated progress, this approach also tends to create or deepen a singer's sense of isolation. The avoidance on the part of a teacher of a conversation about emotions– particularly those commonly related to singing and learning to sing– not only increases the distance between the student and teacher, but often widens the gap between the singer and the perception of his or her vocal abilities and career goals as well.

Chapter Four

Letting the Body Lead:
A Physical-First Approach

Teachers and singers therefore find themselves in a quandary. No matter how they engage with the intellect or emotions, vocal progress and results are not often consistently forthcoming. Where the intellect spins in its unsuccessful attempts to comprehend and control voice production, empowered emotionality gives up in frustration, panic, or despair. Regardless, the proverbial elephant in the room remains.

Yet setting aside these unhelpful dynamics in order to develop the voice can be tremendously challenging, if not virtually impossible, as a conscious endeavor. As in the practice of traditional psychology, reframing cognitions and shifting emotional responses, even when one's desire for change is strong, often requires long-term and intensive efforts. Even then, resolution isn't always forthcoming. Cognitive ideas and cultural agreements about singing, learning to sing, and vocal value– as well as emotions related to these ideas– can be just as resistant to change.

That is not to say that a conversation is without merit. Discussion and communion allow for the sharing of experiences, beliefs, and perceptions that help a teacher to establish a singer's starting point, as well as to build trust and foster the environment necessary for a proper interaction.

However, this interaction is not a verbal inquiry into intellectual, emotional, or vocal issues. Rather, the development of trust and a sense of safety lays a foundation and prepares the way for a series of somatic-based interventions that not only result in effortless vocal learning and knowing, but by their very nature negate the participatory strongholds of the intellect and emotions as well.

The Mirror Neuron System

The success of these interventions is possible thanks to the body's ability to learn in an entirely different manner from that of our cognitive and emotional minds. Thinking and judging fall primarily under the domain of the prefrontal cortices, in which linguistic instruction and intellectual comprehension occur. The amygdala, insula, and other parts of the limbic system are responsible for emotional reconciliation in learning as in life. Physical learning, however, is directed largely by brain cells called the mirror neurons, which utilize observation and– along with the cerebellum– imitation as the primary means of information acquisition and retention.

Just as a baby learns much of its physicality and vocal articulation through this system, so too do singers, dancers, and athletes gain both the elementary and even the advanced knowledge of their crafts. While the intellect can subsequently describe and label, and emotions respond to the observed actions and experiences, it is the physical body that initially experiences and captures the engagements and with repetition (through what is commonly called 'muscle memory') forms them into habits.

The mirror neurons are particularly intriguing for a number of reasons. To begin, they don't discriminate in their 'mirroring'. They merely seek to recreate what we see and hear, regardless of our perceptions of the witnessed actions.

The system is similarly unconcerned with 'how'. One fascinating study found that simply watching someone pick up an object triggered the very same neuro-chemical and muscular activity in a monkey's unmoving body, whether or not it had ever picked up that or any object before. To be clear: even in the absence of action, the monkey's body was physically creating the very engagements it observed.

This aspect of the mirror neuron system has been proven to apply to humans as well. We physically learn not only by doing, but also by merely seeing. And we do so irrespective of our feelings and ideas about the plausibility of the actions we witness.

This should be great news for singers and those longing to sing!

Yet something happens on the way from internal to external expression that changes the flavor of this news for human beings. Physical knowing, before it can be expressed, is first reconciled with our beliefs, thoughts, and feelings about ourselves and the activities we've witnessed. These beliefs and feelings are able to– and so often do– limit what then presents as physically possible, in spite of the fact that we have laid the very neural pathways that ensure success and are, even in stillness, already physically creating the activity.

Accessing Somatic Learning

The challenge, therefore, is not teaching the body the new skill of singing, which it began mastering as a young child through visual and aural observation. Neither is it to change or stop the thoughts and feelings that interfere with the transition from witnessed to expressed action. As we've thus far been exploring, even dedicated efforts to move them to the periphery often prove fruitless. Consider, for example, how successful you have ever been in trying to stop your thoughts or to change your feelings.

The challenge, rather, is to *bypass* them; to somehow cause the mind and emotions to relinquish their powerful hold and control over notions of what is possible so that somatic interrogation, integration, and expression can occur unbothered and unchecked.

In the vocal realm, this is achieved in two ways, both of which reinforce the other and result in positive physical, as well as cognitive and emotional, outcomes.

The first is by appealing directly and exclusively to the body by circumventing the notion that one is singing. This may be accomplished through a series of exercises designed to trick the mind, in which the vocalist is led through the creation of what occur to her as speech and non-musical sounds. Examples of these types of exercises include speaking common phrases with varying levels of emotional intensity, imitating different accents at a variety of volumes, and speaking as if to people at varying distances. Vocal slides, sirens, and nasals (non-musical sound making) may also work. All are ideally approached without a piano or other musical instrument, which– by their use and sometimes, their very presence– tend to encourage vocal inhibition.

In these and similar exercises, in which the perception of singing is absent, the intellect and emotions stay on the sidelines just as they do in walking and talking, leaving the voice able to engage uninterrupted in healthy– and indeed, musical– vocalization. The body captures and records these correct engagements.

The Intuitive Mode

Simply reading the previous paragraphs, the mind often resists accepting or even considering that speech and sirens may be musical, though these types of exercises provide for a highly comparable physiological experience to singing. Therefore, reconciling physical experience with conscious acknowledgment remains problematic, in spite of the fact that the body has already created accurate vocal action.

This is when the second approach to somatic knowing becomes important: a shift in the mind– specifically, a shift in mental focus and perception– that provides for consistent access to effortless and conscious musical vocalization.

This shift is into the intuitive or creative mode familiar to artists, performers, practitioners of meditation, and athletes alike. Often referred to as being in the 'right brain', in 'flow', or in the 'zone', it is a space of tremendous physical, mental, and creative performance potential that simultaneously activates and utilizes numerous and varied regions of the brain.

Common experiences of being in this mode include language faltering, emotions stabilizing, time slowing, and logic and judgment ceasing. These are the optimal conditions for somatic access and learning, and– as you may have noticed– are also the opposite conditions of those previously discussed in the intellect and emotion chapters.

The challenge is not to develop this mode of thinking, as we all have the ability to utilize it. Rather, the challenge is accessing it, which requires the bypassing of the more powerful intellect. Augmented by our educational and cultural systems, its dominance has been reinforced in both technical and creative pursuits from a very early age. In spite of our natural ability to access the intuitive mode at will, we eventually lose familiarity with it for a lack of practice, forming and reinforcing the notion that perhaps we are simply not that creative.

Regardless of this conditioning, accessing the intuitive mode– in a variety of activities– may be accomplished through interventions that distract the intellect from its controlling pursuits long enough for the former to come to the fore.

For example, having a singer vocalize the alphabet on a simple yet unfamiliar melody shifts her mind away from the perceived difficulties of singing and onto attempts to process and conceptually master the new melody. The same may be achieved by having a singer repeat either a voice or piano running through a series of consecutive, non-melodic pitches in very rapid succession.

Preoccupied with trying to get these deceptively tricky exercises right– relearning the ABCs, processing and recreating such rapidly played notes– the mind forgets to 'sing correctly'. (The same is true for certain nasal or consonant-heavy vocalizations that, while melodic, do not occur as musical to the singer.) In each case, the body is able– finally– to engage properly, unimpeded by the judgmental and emotional aspects of the mind.

Results of a Physical-First Approach

Vocal Recognition and Confirmation

At the completion of these and similar exercises (a number of which may be found in *The Art of Singing)*, the vocalist has not only created correct physical action, but has become aware that she was indeed singing. Her mind might insist that it doesn't understand what just happened; her emotions may react to not having control of the effort, yet the singer knows that correct singing occurred.

What's more, the intellect and emotion are recognized as having been unnecessary in what has now been experienced as an effortless physical endeavor.

While a seemingly small and simple step, this realization is a huge leap in both the awareness and tangible experience of what is possible– a first taste of what it can be like to sing and enjoying singing separate of certain thoughts, feelings, and attachments to rewards. Singers who have long relied upon the mind and emotions to dictate action and belief in singing– as well as ideas about the person doing the singing– now begin to realize that vocal outcomes are not inherently connected to these concerns. In this space, the real key and access to optimal performance become obvious: performance itself.

Correct and Cooperative Engagement

Rather than rebel, this and subsequent successes cause the intellect to eventually shift from adversary to ally. Just as it long ago relinquished control over walking and talking, so too may singing be relieved of the intellect's constant inhibiting and interference. No longer attempting to create and comprehend physical action, it can now observe, name, and explain what has returned to a reflexive-first process of development and engagement. Emotions, too, soon begin to widen their focus, responding to real rather than imagined triggers such as lack of preparedness, illness, and injury.

Both remain at the periphery, watching for potential obstacles and barriers to the achievement of vocal and performance success. This distance allows for physical habits to effortlessly form with direct and consistent access to the intuitive realm and somatic learning. At last, mind, emotion, and body have become a team working toward the same end.

Acknowledgment of Cognitive and Emotional Rewards

Having relinquished their former roles, we are now able to objectively consider the long-held positions of the intellect and emotion in the vocal learning process, particularly the reward structures to which they were so tenaciously attached.

First, we can critically observe the intellect's allegiance to the perceptions of power and control. Uncomfortable with a lack of detailed understanding, the mind's unwillingness to surrender physical control has prevented the achievement of the accuracy for which it so longs. The desire to be in control of the learning process and to engage perfectly has been too powerful, more so than the conscious desire to sing well.

We now also clearly see the reward of emotion as the perceived avoidance of failure through its commitment to non-change. For a host of reasons– including past experiences, future imaginings, present insecurities, and messages from the intellect about the importance of remaining in control– emotions have come to the fore at even minor indications of movement away from stasis. Regardless of the gap between where a singer is and where she wants to be, feared notions of change have until now remained more powerful than the desire for progress. Thus, the reward of stagnation has been greater than the risk of moving outside of her vocal, performance, or career comfort zones.

Through the perspective granted by the achievement of successful, integrated vocal engagements, we are now able to objectively marvel at these forces that have sought to keep us safe and in control, in spite of their inability to do so.

Yet while they no longer stand in the way of practice and performance progress, they do not disappear. On the contrary; just as performance anxiety may always make the heart race and the mouth go dry, fear continues to insist upon the certainty of its fatalistic views. The intellect remains sure of its power to manipulate outcome.

Fortunately, rather than re-inspiring control, panic, or belief in their accuracy, these voices are now recognized as part of the vocal condition as they are the human condition: cognitive and emotional mechanisms which, in spite of their design to protect us, often protect us from the very progress we so desire. Thankfully we are now able to acknowledge their well-intentioned– though inaccurate– aims, and to no longer to allow them to hinder performance.

Chapter Five

Beyond Singing:
Implications for Living

Extending our focus, the question arises whether this type of breakthrough is possible in personal pursuits as well. The answer is a definitive yes. Just as the intellect and emotion– when improperly empowered– are barriers to effortless vocal action, so too are they obstacles in non-musical ways of creating, relating, and being.

A Plan of Action

As we've discussed, in singing the intellect is unqualified to determine what is possible as well as how those possibilities might best be achieved. The same is true in life; our thoughts are often incapable of ascertaining and helping us to manifest our personal potential. What is possible and what is practical become confused– a confusion reflected in and confirmed by language.

(So accustomed are we to the blending of these ideas that many of us have forgotten the true nature of each. As a clarification, what is possible is objectively achievable irrespective of how difficult or improbable it may appear. Practical, on the other hand, is always in relation to an established– and usually restrictive– custom, idea, or expectation.)

Given this confusion, our cultural beliefs and personal judgments create, confirm, and maintain the status quo, reinforcing our learned standards of what is normal, acceptable, and reasonable. Unless we challenge these notions and distinguish between them, we remain unable to allow for a more flexible and higher standard of excellence, adventure, and bold daring– to see, and eventually live into, what is truly possible.

Similarly, as emotion limits movement toward the physical fluidity and personal vulnerability required for new and improved vocal engagements, so too does it arise and halt action toward the unknown in life. Regardless of how powerful the dream of and longing for a new reality may be, our feelings often keep us tethered to what we perceive as safe, rather than moving in the direction of our desires.

In spite of these limitations, we fortunately have access, as we do in singing, to a system that empowers and indeed enables us to create new and improved outcomes in our lives: identifying our true (rather than stasis-related and practical) desires, making a commitment to achieving them, and taking action.

In singing, a shift into the intuitive mode is what halts the interfering aspects of the intellect and emotion, allowing for the uninhibited physical creation of what the mirror neuron witness.

In life, it is action– given by intention and commitment– that circumvents the dominance of our thoughts and feelings and confirms our ability to create.

Challenges to Engagement

While an uncomplicated system, it is not a simple one. For every effort toward action, logic and reason spring to the fore to contradict the notion that new outcomes may be so easily created. Emotions personalize the seeming impossibilities, dissuading, preventing, and even crippling us in our endeavors toward forward movement. Action is therefore halted, often before it is even begun.

The Current Psychological Paradigm

These perceived obstacles are supported and confirmed not only by personal experience, but by academic psychology and professional counseling as well. As in the study and teaching of singing, intellectual understanding is often confused with and seen as a prerequisite for progress, becoming the therapeutic goal prior to or even in lieu of action. Large periods of time are therefore dedicated to the consideration of and negotiation with cognitions and emotions that have little interest in being altered; cognitions and emotions that have in fact created and endorsed the very obstacles one is seeking to change.

What's more, our comprehension-directed focus on the past as a gateway to a healthy present and desired future tends to further empower our reasons for why we are the way we are, rather than encourage the objective plausibility of and path toward achieving our goals. The honoring of, if not reverence for, one's history is often so powerful that it is considered an anomaly, if not an impossibility, for humans to act independently of their pasts' influence. This sets a very certain, though inaccurate, standard for what is actually possible both in one's life and in the counseling dynamic.

That is not to say that our histories are irrelevant. On the contrary; our beliefs and emotions are assembled– as they are in singing– according to our past experiences and carried forward with the well-intentioned, though often misguided, hopes of protecting us in the present.

The point, rather, is that the presence and content of our thoughts and feelings are unrelated to what is actually possible, as well as to our ability to take action.

In the singing realm, this is clear. Spending years or even months considering why a technique might have been incorrectly formed or one's thoughts and feelings about the matter is unfathomable. Healthy performance in the present is the only goal; a goal– as we have seen– that neither requires nor is necessarily helped by intellectual comprehension, personal agreement, or emotional reconciliation prior to engagement.

Commitment and Reward in Personal Performance

The same is true in the arena of personal performance. It is not a lack of comprehension, incorrect beliefs, or emotional overwhelm that necessarily prevents us from achieving the outcomes we so desire. Insight and calm are often gained in the counseling arena to little or no tangible or lasting effect.

Rather, as in singing, it is a greater commitment to some form of stasis– supported by a reward– that prevents us from accomplishing our aims. This reward generally involves a measure of, or full relief from, responsibility for outcomes– or at the very least, responsibility for one's reactions to them.

The suggestion of the acceptance of responsibility as a primary gateway to desired results is an uncommon and often resisted one. Myriad explanations are proffered for why taking action prior to gaining understanding or achieving confidence would be unsustainable, if not unwise.

Yet these explanations stem from a paradigm that tends to focus on matters of right, wrong, fair, and unfair as an important component of providing personal resolution. Unfortunately, by subscribing to this view, we create a notion of how the world *should* be and thus, create ourselves as victims within it for any perceived disparity.

Armed with this excuse to not honor or even make commitments in life, our power to create is whisked away; a power we trade for the greater reward of explaining why circumstances, people (including ourselves), and life should be or should have been different. In response, thoughts and emotions present as action-stopping variations on the themes of anxiety, blame, expectation, entitlement, and attachment, which then become the focus for the intellectual exercise of much therapy.

From Intention to Reality

That is not to say that therapy doesn't work, or that abuse, neglect, and trauma occur without consequence. On the contrary; there is a certain impact for every step we take in the world, and the ties between experience, interpretation, and effectiveness are neither always clear nor stable. Intellectual and emotional therapeutic interventions in these situations can be enormously helpful. As well, whether for nurture, nature, or a combination of the two, inefficiencies in mental functioning may certainly impair the structures required to manage, test, and reconstruct both cognitive and actual boundaries.

That said, the majority of us are graced with the opportunity through action to claim the life we desire, in spite of whatever may have come before and the current pleadings of our thoughts and feelings; an opportunity confirmed by recent research in, among other areas, positive psychology, transformative learning, and neural plasticity. Newer models of short-term psychological treatments, reality and action-directed cognitive-behavioral therapies, and life and personal performance coaching support these findings and are becoming commensurately more popular.

In this view, failures in life are only those of imagination and effort. By choosing what it is we want, making a commitment to attaining it, and taking action toward that end we begin to create new evidence for and thus, a shifted perspective of what is actually possible. New feelings and thoughts greet this evidence and shifted perspective, setting in motion the ongoing creation of an entirely new awareness and eventually, a new reality.

As in the singing realm, in life we are each presented with the options of conceptualization or creation, of ambivalence or action; to live a life of intention and design or to focus on why we do not have and can't seem to get what we want.

The choice is ours.

References

Chapter 1: Introduction

Hamady, J. (2009). *The Art of Singing: Discovering and Developing Your True Voice.* Milwaukee, WI: Hal Leonard Corporation.

Chapter 2: Intellect

Ax, A. F. (1964). Goals and methods of psychophysiology. *Psychophysiology, 1,* 8–25.

Blakemore, S. J., Frith, U. (2005). *The Learning Brain: Lessons for Education.* New York, NY: Wiley-Blackwell.

Calais-Germain, B. (2006). *Anatomy of Breathing.* Seattle, WA: Eastland Press.

Cross, I.C. (2001). Music, mind and evolution. *Psychology of Music,* 29, 95–102.

Csikszentmihalyi, M. (2008). *Flow: The Psychology of Optimal Experience.* New York, NY: Harper Perennial Modern Classics.

DeLiège, I. and Sloboda, J.A. (ed.) (1997). *Perception and Cognition of Music.* Hove, UK: Psychology Press.

Edwards, B. (1998). *Drawing on the Right Side of the Brain: Enhancing Creativity and Artistic Confidence.* New York, NY: Tarcher/Putnam.

Feltz, D. L., Landers, D. M. (1983). The effects of mental practice on motor skill learning and performance: A meta-analysis. *Journal of Sport Psychology, 5.* 25-57.

Fix, James D. (2002). *Neuroanatomy*. Hagerstown, MD: Lippincott Williams & Wilkins.

Ginsburg, C. (1999). Body-image, movement and consciousness: examples from a somatic practice in the Feldenkrais Method. *Journal of Consciousness Studies, 6.* 79-91.

Hargreaves, D.J. and North, A.C. (1999). The functions of music in everyday life: redefining the social in music psychology. *Psychology of Music, 27,* 71–83.

Levitin, D. (2007). *This is your Brain on Music: The Science of a Human Obsession.* New York, NY: Plume/Penguin.

Lhermitte, F., Pillon, B. and Serdaru, M. (1986), Human autonomy and the frontal lobes. Part I: Imitation and utilization behavior: A neuropsychological study of 75 patients. *Annals of Neurology, 19,* 326–334.

Lyons, J. (1981). Why human development requires more than one mode of experience. *Journal for the Theory of Social Behaviour, 11,* 167–188.

MacDonald, R.A., Miell, D.E. (2000). Creativity and music education: the impact of social variables. *International Journal of Music Education, 36,* 58–68.

Machens, C., Romo, R., Brody, C. (2010). Functional, but not anatomical, separation of "what" and "when" in prefrontal cortex. *The Journal of Neuroscience, 30,* 350-360.

Oehler, S., Hanley, J. (2009), Perspectives of popular music pedagogy in practice: an introduction. *Journal of Popular Music Studies, 21,* 2–19.

Perkins, W. H., Kent, R. D. (1986). *Functional Anatomy of Speech, Language, and Hearing.* Boston, MA: College-Hill Press.

Pinker, S. (2009). *How the Mind Works.* New York, NY: Norton.

Ristad, E. (1982). *A Soprano on her Head: Right-side-up Reflections on Life and Other Performances.* Moab, UT: Real People Press.

Saladin, K. (2010). *Anatomy and Physiology: The Unity of Form and Function.* Ontario, Canada: McGraw-Hill Science.

Shuter-Dyson, R., Gabriel, C. (1981). *The Psychology of Musical Ability, 2nd ed.* London, UK: Methuen.

Titze, I. R. (2000). *Principles of Voice Production.* Salt Lake City, UT: National Center for Voice and Speech.

Titze, I. R. (2010). *Fascinations with the Human Voice.* Salt Lake City, UT: National Center for Voice and Speech.

Tolley, D. (2008). *A Contemporary Music Program: A Music Industry Program for Today's Colleges and Universities.* Saarbrücken, Germany: VDM Verlag.

Trevarthen, C. (1999). Musicality and the intrinsic motive pulse: evidence from human psychobiology and infant communication. *Musicae Scientiae, Special Issue,* 155–215.

Tymoczko, D. (2008), Scale theory, serial theory and voice leading. *Music Analysis, 27,* 1–49.

Zull, J. E. (2002). *The Art of Changing the Brain.* Sterling, VA: Stylus Publishing.

Chapter 3: Emotion

Amsel, A. (2006). *Frustration Theory: An Analysis of Dispositional Learning and Memory.* Cambridge, UK: Cambridge University Press.

Aronson, E. (2007). *The Social Animal (10th Edition).* New York, NY: Worth Publishers.
Cameron, J., Pierce, W. D. (2002). *Rewards and Intrinsic Motivation: Resolving the Controversy.* London, UK: Bergin & Garvey.

Corr, P. J. (2010), Automatic and controlled processes in behavioural control: Implications for personality psychology. *European Journal of Personality, 24,* 376–403.

Dejonckere, P. H. (2001). *Occupational Voice: Care and Cure.* Amsterdam, The Netherlands: Kugler.

Dweck, C.S. (1999). *Self-Theories: Their Role in Motivation, Personality and Development.* Hove, UK: Psychology Press.

Freund, P. E. S. (1990), The expressive body: a common ground for the sociology of emotions and health and illness. *Sociology of Health & Illness, 12,* 452–477.

Hamady, J. (2009). *The Art of Singing: Discovering and Developing your True Voice.* Milwaukee, WI: Hal Leonard Corporation.

LeDoux, J. (1996). *The Emotional Brain: The Mysterious Underpinnings of Emotional Life.* New York, NY: Touchstone.

Lock, M. (1993). *Cultivating the Body: Anthropologies and Epistemologies of Bodily Practice and Knowledge.* Quebec, Canada: McGill University Press.

Sanderson, P. M. (1989). Verbalizable knowledge and skilled task performance: association, dissociation, and mental models. *Journal of Experimental Psychology: Learning, Memory, and Cognition, 15,* 729-747.

Shweder, R. A., Goodnow, J. J., Hatano, G., LeVine, R. A., Markus, H. R. and Miller, P. J. (2007). The cultural psychology of development: one mind, many mentalities. In W. Damon & R. M. Lehrer (Eds.), *Handbook of Child Psychology, Volume 1: Theoretical Models of Human Development.* Hoboken, NJ: John Wiley & Sons.

Storr, A. (1992). *Music and the Mind.* New York, NY: Ballantine Books.

Chapter 4: Letting the Body Lead: A Physical-First Approach

Ax, A. F. (1964). Goals and methods of psychophysiology. *Psychophysiology, 1,* 8–25.

Badets, A., Blandin, Y., Shea, C. H. (2006). Intention in motor learning through observation. *Experimental Psychology, 59,* 377-386.

Bankart, C. P. (1996). *Talking Cures: A History of Western and Eastern Psychotherapies.* Florence, KY: Brooks Cole.

Barry, N., Hallam, S. (2002). Practicing. In R. Parncutt & G. E. McPherson (Eds.), *The Science and Psychology of Music Performance: Creative Strategies for Teaching and Learning.* New York, NY: Oxford University Press.

Brodal, P. (2010). *The Central Nervous System: Structure and Function.* New York, NY: Oxford University Press USA.

Cross, E. S., Kraemer, D. J., Hamilton, A., Kelley, W. M., Grafton, S. T. (2009). Sensitivity of the action observation network to physical and observational learning. *Cerebral Cortex, 19,* 315-326.

Csikszentmihalyi, M. (2008). *Flow: The Psychology of Optimal Experience.* New York, NY: Harper Perennial Modern Classics.

Davis, M., & Whalen, P. J. (2001). The amygdala: vigilance and emotion. *Molecular Psychiatry,* 6, 13–34.

Edwards, B. (1986). *Drawing on the Artist Within: A Practical Guide to Increasing Your Creative Powers.* New York, NY: Fireside.

Jaworski, J. (1996). *Synchronicity: The Inner Path of Leadership.* San Francisco, CA: Berrett Koehler Publishers.

Keysers, C., Fadiga, L. (Eds.), (2010). *The Mirror Neuron System: A Special Issue of Social Neuroscience.* London, UK: Psychology Press.

Lehrer, J. (2011, January, 19). The Neuroscience of Music. *Wired Magazine.*

Overy, K., Molnar-Szakacs, I. (2009). Being together in time: musical experience and the mirror neuron system. *Music Perception, 26,* 489-504.

Pinker, S. (2007). *The Stuff of Thought: Language as a Window into Human Nature.* New York, NY: Penguin.

Rizzolatti, G. (2005). The mirror neuron system and its function in humans. *Anatomy and Embryology, 210,* 419-421.

Rizzolatti, G., Fogassi, L., Gallese, V. (2001). Neurophysiological mechanisms underlying the understanding and imitation of action. *Nature Reviews Neuroscience 2,* 661-670.

Rogers, Carl. (1961). *On Becoming a Person.* Boston, MA: Houghton Mifflin.

Seligman, M. (1995). The effectiveness of psychotherapy. *American Psychologist, 50,* 965-974. Washington DC: American Psychological Association, Inc.

Tobacyk, J. J., Downs, A. (1998). Personal construct threat and irrational beliefs as cognitive predictors of increases in musical performance anxiety. *Journal of Personal Social Psychology, 83,* 678-692.

Velichkovskiĭ, B. M., Rumbaugh, D. M. (1996). *Communicating Meaning: The Evolution and Development of Language.* London, UK: Psychology Press.

Wilson, G. D. (2002). *Psychology for Performing Artists.* London, UK: Whurr Publishers.

Chapter 5: Beyond Singing: Implications for Living

Ansermet, F., Magistretti, P. (2007). *Biology of Freedom: Neural Plasticity, Experience, and the Unconscious.* New York, NY: Other Press.

Bandura, A. (1986). *Social Foundations of Thought and Action: A Social Cognitive Theory.* Englewoord Cliffs, NJ: Prentice Hall.

Bankart, C. P. (1996). *Talking Cures: A History of Western and Eastern Psychotherapies.* Florence, KY: Brooks Cole.

Barge, J. K., Little, M. (2008). A discursive approach to skillful activity. *Communication Theory, 18,* 505–534.

Blakemore, S. J., Frith, U. (2005). *The Learning Brain: Lessons for Education.* New York, NY: Wiley-Blackwell.

Cameron, J., Pierce, W. D. (2002). *Rewards and Intrinsic Motivation: Resolving the Controversy.* London, UK: Bergin & Garvey.

Csikszentmihalyi, M. (1997). *Creativity: Flow and the Psychology of Discovery and Invention.* New York, NY: Harper Perennial.

Dilts, R., Davis, D. (1980). *Neuro-linguistic Programming: Volume I (The Study of the Structure of Subjective Experience).* Capitola, CA: Meta Publications.

Dweck, C.S. (1999). *Self-theories: Their Role in Motivation, Personality and Development.* Hove, UK: Psychology Press.

Ellis, A. (2001). *Overcoming Destructive Beliefs, Feelings, and Behaviors: New Directions for Rational Emotive Behavior Therapy.* Amherst, NY: Prometheus Books.

Freud, S. (1920). *Introduction to Psychoanalysis: Lectures.* New York, NY: Boni and Liveright Publishers.

Freud, S. (1923). *The Ego and the Id.* New York, NY: W. W. Norton and Company.

Glasser, W. (1999). *Choice Theory: A New Psychology of Personal Freedom.* New York, NY: Harper Perennial.

Hayes, S. C., Barnes-Holmes, D., Roche, B. (2001). *Relational Frame Theory: A Post Skinnerian Account of Human Language and Cognition.* New York, NY: Kluwer Academic/Plenum Publishers.

Hayes, S. C., Strosahl, K. D., Wilson, K. G. (1999). *Acceptance and Commitment Therapy: An Experiential Approach to Behavior Change.* New York, NY: Guilford Press.

Hendricks, G. (2001). *Conscious Living: How to Create a Life of Your Own Design.* New York, NY: Harper.

LeDoux, J. (1996). *The Emotional Brain: The Mysterious Underpinnings of Emotional Life.* New York, NY: Touchstone.

Peterson, C. (2006). *A Primer in Positive Psychology.* New York, NY: Oxford University Press USA.

Pineles, S. L., Mineka, S. (2005). Attentional biases to internal and external sources of potential threat in social anxiety. *Journal of Abnormal Psychology, 114,* 314-318.

Ridley, M. (2003). *Nature via Nurture: Genes, Experience, and What Makes us Human.* New York, NY: Harper Perennial.

Seligman, M. (1995). The effectiveness of psychotherapy. *American Psychologist, 50,* 965-974. Washington DC: American Psychological Association, Inc.

Skinner, N., Brewer, N. (2002). The dynamics of threat and challenge appraisals prior to stressful achievement events. *Journal of Personality and Social Psychology, 51,* 779-782.

Sullivan, H. S. (1984). *Personal Psychopathology: Early Formulations.* New York, NY: W. W. Norton & Company.

Szasz, T. (2010). *The Myth of Mental Illness: Foundations of a Theory of Personal Conduct.* New York, NY: Harper Perennial.

Tallman, K., Bohart, A. C. (1999). The client as a common factor: clients as self-healers. In M. A. Hubble, B. L. Duncan, & S. D. Miller (Eds.), *The heart and soul of change: What works in therapy.* Washington, DC: American Psychological Association.

Yiend, J. (2004). *Cognition, Emotion, and Psychopathology: Theoretical, Empirical, and Clinical Directions.* Cambridge, UK: Cambridge University Press.

Acknowledgements

There is none so great as he who is willing to defer to the wisdom and guidance of others.

This book is dedicated to the many wonderful people who have taught me this principle and encourage me to honor it.

My sincere thanks go to
Dr. Tracy Garrett
Dr. James Fallon
Dr. Jessica Morris
Cassidy Hooker and
Melissa Guttman
for their guidance, input, counsel, and editing

as well as to
my husband, my family, my friends, my clients,
my colleagues and my community
without whom
I simply would not be
the person I am today.

Praise for
The Art of Singing: Discovering and Developing Your True Voice

What an incredible book... I've read it twice!
Daniel Levitin, author, "The World in Six Songs" and
"This is Your Brain on Music"

In Jennifer Hamady's extremely thoughtful and commendably helpful how-to guide, she writes... with indisputable common sense, about singing from a different, if not entirely radical, perspective.
David Finkle, Back Stage

It's "The Artist's Way", "The Four Agreements", and "Drawing on the Right Side of the Brain" all rolled into one. A new book, author, and force to be reckoned with.
Don Davis, Variety

Words cannot express how much your book has done for me as a singer and as a music educator. Thank you...
Mimi Parroco, New York University

She's written the singer's version of "The Secret". Oprah would be proud!
Clair Reilly-Roe, Singer/Songwriter, NYC

I LOVE IT! I'm currently in Mamma Mia on Broadway and your book is changing the way I work. Thank you for writing something so brilliant!
Monica Kapoor

Thank you for writing this book. My heart is leaping with joy that there are other people out there thinking like this. It has given me a sense of belonging and direction for my teaching, and has been a huge help to my students.
Liz Johnson, Professor, Blair School of Music
Vanderbilt University

I came to Jennifer to rediscover how to sing. What she helped me find was my voice. There is no greater gift. This book should be on everyone's list of must-reads.
Charles Day
President, The Lookinglass Consultancy

Jennifer's book simply confirms her abilities in discerning the fundamentals of life. Powerfully insightful, her treatment of fear not only has immediate application but revolutionary impact, as she has identified the core problems that undermine the full performance of so many people. There is no doubt in my mind that the book will have enormous positive impact on a wide cross section of people.
Dr. Amii-Omara Ottunu
Chair, UNESCO Institute of Human Rights

Printed in Great Britain
by Amazon